THE WORLD TO

New Global Economies

Colin Hynson

W
FRANKLIN WATTS
LONDON • SYDNEY

First published in 2008
by Franklin Watts

Copyright © Franklin Watts 2008

Franklin Watts
338 Euston Road
London NW1 3BH

Franklin Watts Australia
Level 17/207 Kent Street
Sydney, NSW 2000

All rights reserved.

Editor: Jeremy Smith
Design: Simon Borrough
Art director: Jonathan Hair

Picture credits: Action Press/Rex Features: 32. Trygve Bolstad/Panos: 19. Stefan Boness/Panos: 21. Charcrit Boonsom/Robert Harding/Rex Features: 9. Mary Evans PL: 12t. Grace/Keystone USA/Rex Features: 12b. Sari Gustafsson/Rex Features: 26. Michael Harvey/Panos: 28. Mark Henley/Panos: 6, 20, 22, 37. Rhodri Jones /Panos: 39. Natalia Kolesnikova.Epsilon/Panos: 34. Christiana Laruffa/Rex Features: 16t. Atul Loke/Panos: 14, 15. Jenny Matthews/Panos: 18. Pierre Merimee/Corbis: 40. Fernando Moleres/Panos: 31. Rex Features: 10, 35. Qilai Shen/Panos: 13, 38. Jacob Silberberg/Panos: 23. Sipa Press/Rex Features: 11, 17, 27, 33, 36, 41. Chris Stowers/Panos: 30. Ian Teh/Panos: 29. Rainer Unkel/vario images/Alamy: 25.

Every attempt has been made to clear copyright. Should there be any inadvertent omission please apply to the publisher for rectification.

A CIP catalogue record for this book is available from the British Library.

Dewey number: 629.47

ISBN 978 0 7496 8103 6

Printed in Hong Kong

Franklin Watts is a division of Hachette Children's Books, an Hachette Livre UK company
www.hachettelivre.co.uk

Contents

What is a New Global Economy?	8
The rise of New Global Economies	10
New Global Economy - China	12
New Global Economy - India	14
Populations in the New Global Economies	16
Education in the New Global Ecomomies	18
Rich and poor	20
Workers' rights	22
Child labour	24
Politics and human rights	26
Environmental concerns	28
The growth of the city	30
New world powers	32
Looking for resources	34
Global culture	36
The impact on the developed world	38
The future	40
Glossary	42
Weblinks	43
Index	44

What is a New Global Economy?

For hundreds of years, the world economy has been dominated by Europe and the United States. Most of the world's goods were manufactured in these areas and people living in other parts of the world had no choice but to buy these goods from them. In the past 20 years, that has begun to change and several countries have emerged as competitors to the Western economies.

A map showing the G8 (green) countries, and the major New Global Economies (blue).

The G8

At the moment the most powerful economies in the world are Canada, France, Germany, Italy, Japan, Russia, the United Kingdom and the United States. Together they control over 65% of the entire wealth of the world. They are known as the G8 (Group of Eight) and the governments of these countries have met together every year since 1975 to discuss the world economy and world politics. Russia joined the G8 in 1998.

Who are the New Global Economies?

There is some disagreement about this. In 2005, the British Prime Minister, Tony Blair, invited the five countries that were seen as the most important New Global Economies to meet with the G8. These countries were Brazil, China, India, Mexico and South Africa, now known as G8+5. Previous to this, the G20 was formed in 1999. This group of developed and

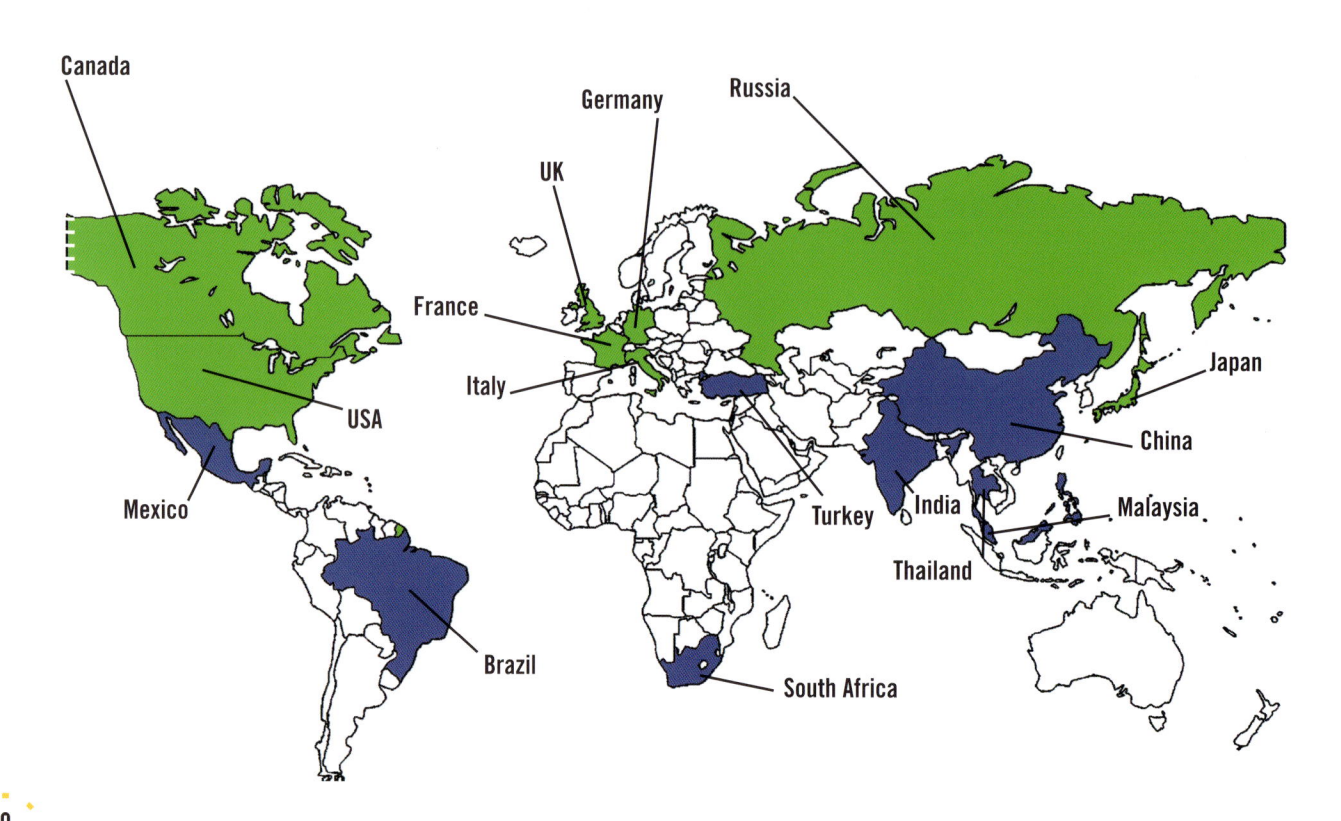

'If this projection holds, **Brazil will have overtaken Italy's economy** by 2025, and France's by 2031. Russia will pass the UK in 2027, and Germany in 2028. In fact, the report suggests that by mid-century only the United States and Japan will rank among the world's top six economies.'

Paul Kennedy, Professor of History at Yale University, talking about the predictions made by Goldman Sachs investment bank about the future of the world's economies

developing countries includes the G8+5 and seven more economically important countries like South Korea, Saudi Arabia and Turkey.

BRICs and BRIMCs

In 2003 the bank, Goldman Sachs, produced a report on the economies that would become the most important by 2050. The writers of the report called them BRICs (Brazil, Russia, India and China). Mexico was added to this list later to create the BRIMC. Most people agree that the New Global Economies should include Brazil, India and China but there is still a debate about which other countries should be added to this list.

THOUGHT BOX

How much do you think it will change the world if the BRIMC countries become more economically powerful over the next 40 years, while other countries decline in economic importance?

By 2050, many economists think that countries such as Russia (right) will be among the richest in the world.

9

The rise of the New Global Economies

The former president of the USA, Ronald Reagan, with the former British prime minister, Margaret Thatcher.

THOUGHT BOX

There are people who think that the 'Cold War' (see opposite) was a good thing because there was less uncertainty in the world. You were either on one side or the other. What do you think of that idea?

The 1980s saw political and economic changes around the world. In particular, the rise in free markets and free trade led directly to the rise of the New Global Economies. Alongside these changes were great improvements in information technology. These allowed economies around the world to work together more closely.

The rise of the free market

In 1981, the citizens of the United States of America elected a new president, Ronald Reagan. He promised to make the American economy as free as possible from state control. Along with the prime minister of the United Kingdom, Margaret Thatcher, President Reagan believed that state control of the UK and US economies (the number of companies owned and run by the state rather than by private business) should be drastically reduced. Their ideas spread to many countries, including China and India. Now companies were allowed to expand at home and abroad without interference from the state.

'From France to the Philippines, from Jamaica to Japan, from Malaysia to Mexico, from Sri Lanka to Singapore, privatisation is on the move… The policies we have pioneered are catching on in country after country.'

Margaret Thatcher, British Prime Minister, 1986

The fall of communism

After World War II (1939–45), there were two superpowers: the capitalist United States and the communist Soviet Union. These two countries, along with their allies, fought what was called the 'Cold War' for over three decades. In 1989, communist countries in Eastern Europe saw their governments fall as people demanded free elections and free markets. One year later, the Soviet Union itself broke up into 15 different countries, the most important of which was Russia. Many, but not all, of these new countries also embraced free markets as a way of changing their old state-controlled economies.

Information technology

During the 1980s and 1990s, it became easier and easier for people around the world to contact each other instantly, by phone, email or the Internet. This meant that different economies around the world could work closely with each other and they became much more interconnected.

Hundreds of people flood through the Berlin Wall following its collapse in 1989 to escape from communist East Germany into capitalist West Germany.

New Global Economy - China

Left: An illustration from the 1950s showing the Chinese communist leader Mao Zedong.

Below: Under Deng Xiaoping, China began to open up parts of its country to foreign investment, transforming the nation.

The chances are that something you bought recently was made in China. This might be an electrical good, like a television or a mobile phone, or a pair of trainers. The Chinese economy is growing fast and has become one of the world's biggest manufacturer of goods. This change is even more amazing as only 30 years ago, China was a very poor country.

The death of Mao

From 1949, China was ruled by the Chinese Communist Party under the leadership of Mao Zedong. Mao believed that the Chinese economy should be strictly controlled by the state. His economic policies meant that the Chinese people suffered a great deal. By the time of Mao's death in 1976, China could only just produce enough food to feed its people. With his death, a power struggle within the Chinese Communist Party began. A politician called Deng Xiaoping won through and China set off on a new path.

From Mao to Deng

When Deng Xiaoping came to power in 1976, China was technologically 30 years behind the Western world and China's people did not have anything like the standard of living of people in Europe and North America.

THOUGHT BOX

Do you think that Deng Xiaoping was right, since by loosening state control of the economy, China has grown in wealth and power?

To tackle this problem, Deng began to loosen state control over the economy. He welcomed foreign companies to set up factories and other businesses in Special Economic Zones around the coast of China. These zones, along with a large and cheap workforce, attracted many of the world's largest companies to China. By the end of the 1990s, China had become one of the most important economies in the world.

Hong Kong

China also benefitted from regaining control of Hong Kong. This area had been controlled by the British from 1842 and they had turned it into a major world financial centre. In 1997, Hong Kong was returned to China and it has remained a very important financial centre, generating much wealth for China.

A view of the Jin Mao Tower and the Pudong Financial District from the top of the Shanghai World Financial Centre, China.

'It doesn't matter if a cat is **black or white**, so long as it catches mice.'
Deng Xiaoping explains why it is good to have a free market in a communist country

New Global Economy - India

In the 1770s, India had the second-largest economy in the entire world. Yet by the 1970s, it had become a poor and undeveloped country. This was partly due to the way that the British ruled India during the 19th century and also due to the economic policies of the Indian government after independence. In the early 1990s, things began to change and India is now emerging as a major economic power once again.

Independence

Along with Pakistan, India became independent from Britain in 1947. India's new leaders were influenced by socialists who believed that the economy should be controlled and planned by the state. The government started a series of five-year plans in which the economy had to meet targets set by the government. Many industries were also owned by the state and there were restrictions on goods going in or out of the country. Businesses were controlled by what was called the 'Licence Raj'. These were complicated regulations that all businesses had to follow in India.

'Narasimha Rao ... opened the economy... dismantled import controls, lowered customs duties, and devalued the currency ... virtually abolished licensing controls on private investment, dropped tax rates, and broke public sector monopolies. **We felt as though our second independence had arrived.**' **Gurcharan Das**, an Indian businessman and writer

THOUGHT BOX

Why do you think that the early leaders of India wanted to control the Indian economy so closely?

Until recently, India has been a poor country based around its agriculture.

Visitors arrive at India's impressive new airport, for the capital, Mumbai.

Opening up India

In 1991, the newly elected prime minister, Narasimha Rao, and his finance minister, Manmohan Singh, began a series of reforms to change the Indian economy and help to lift many Indians out of poverty. He got rid of the 'Licence Raj' very quickly so that there was far less regulation of Indian businesses. Many parts of the Indian economy that were actually owned by the state, such as the banks, were sold off into private hands. The government also allowed foreign companies to start working in India and, as in China, Special Economic Zones were created to attract foreign companies into India.

The Indian economy today

Since 2003, India has become one of the fastest-growing economies in the world. It is now a major centre for telecommunications and for the computer industry. The building of a new road that will link all of the most important cities in India will also help to push India's economy forward.

Populations in the New Global Economies

Many commentators on the New Global Economies point to the fact that they all have very large populations. This can provide a large workforce for any business setting up in one of these countries and as people in the New Global Economies get wealthier then they will consume many more goods. Many companies are looking at China as an increasingly important place to sell their goods.

Large populations

The four main new global economies – Brazil, Russia, India and China – have some of the world's largest populations. In April 2008, China had about 1,323,286,000 people and it is the most populated country in the world. The second-biggest country by population is India, with about 1,131,644,000 people in 2008. India's population is expected to overtake China's by 2030. Brazil has the fifth-largest population in the world with 186,580,000 people in 2008. Russia has about 142,000,000 people and is the ninth-largest in the world.

THOUGHT BOX

Some experts believe that countries in Europe and North America need more young people in order to compete with the New Global Economies. Should these countries encourage more immigration of young people?

A busy shopping mall in the chief town of the the province of Shaanxi, China.

A map of the world drawn according to population size rather than geographical extent. It illustrates the contrast between the New Global Economies and the G8 countries.

Young and old

One of the problems that is facing countries in Europe and North America is that the average age of their populations is growing older as people live longer and have fewer children. This means that in the future there will be fewer young people. Young people are needed to work, pay taxes and create a country's wealth.

The New Global Economies have much younger populations. Over 25% of all Brazilians are under 14 years old, 32% of all Indians are under 15 years old. China has a slightly older population because of its 'one-child' policy. This was started in the early 1970s as a way of controlling a rapidly growing population. Less than 20% of Chinese are under 14 years of age but that still adds up to over 270 million young people – more than enough for China's future workforce.

'Ageing has been **a hidden problem** in China for some time. Since 1980, the elderly population has been growing faster than the average of the world and Asia. Yet ageing was not considered a serious problem 20 years ago, because there was a large pool of young people aged 0-15 who rapidly replaced the elderly exiting the labour force.' **Helen (Hong) Qiao**, an economist with the bank Goldman Sachs, 2006

Crowds of young people gather on a bathing beach in Dalian, China.

Education in the New Global Economies

If the New Global Economies are going to compete successfully against the established economies then they must make sure that their people are educated. This is especially important if they are going to use new technologies to expand their economies. However, providing education for such large populations is very expensive. For many of the poor in these countries, educating children is a luxury that few can afford.

Levels of Literacy

Countries such as Britain and the United States have a literacy rate of about 99%. The literacy levels in most of the new global economies are lower than this. India has a literacy rate of about 61%, China has a literacy rate of just over 90% and Brazil has a literacy rate of about 88%. In many of these countries women receive far less education than men. In India only 54% of women are literate while in China the figure is about 86%. Both countries are trying to increase the number of women who can read and write.

Children at secondary school in Porto De Moz, Brazil.

A map showing global literacy levels in 2007.

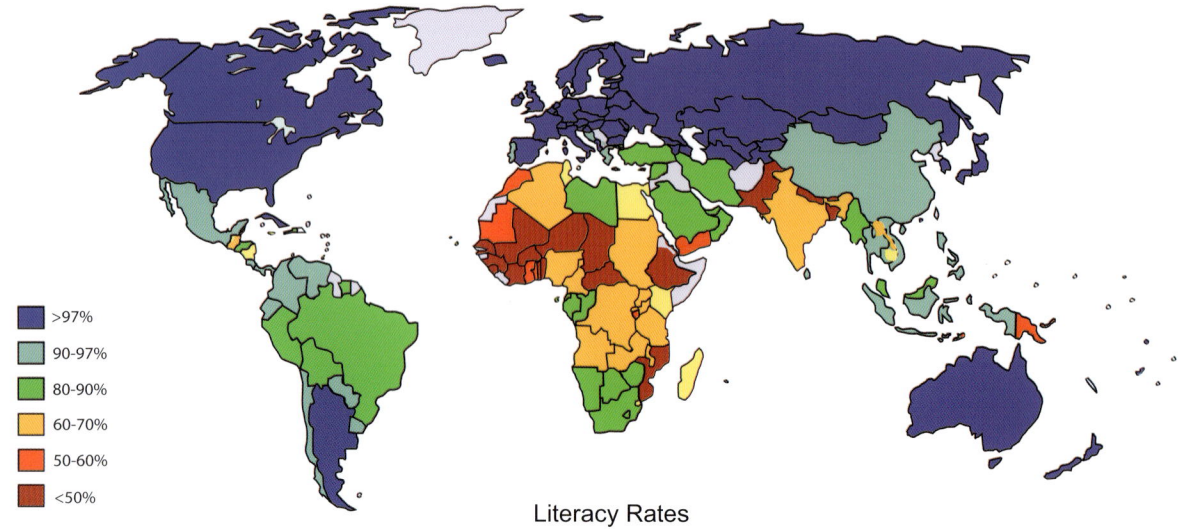

- \>97%
- 90-97%
- 80-90%
- 60-70%
- 50-60%
- <50%

Literacy Rates

Higher education

The New Global Economies need to have many more young people who are experts in various fields, especially engineering and computer science. India is creating more university places for people to study computing and telecommunications because the government wants the Indian economy to become a world leader in high-tech industries. In 1999 in China only 10% of young people went to university but by 2006 this had grown to over 26%. Universities are springing up across China to meet the need for a well-educated workforce.

THOUGHT BOX

Many universities in Europe and North America are setting up new universities in India and China. Why are they doing this and whom will it benefit?

Graduation day for students from the Physics Department of Tsinghua University, China.

'China is now the largest higher education system in the world: **it awards more** university degrees than the USA and India combined.' **Mike Baker**, Educational Journalist for the BBC

Rich and poor

THOUGHT BOX
Do you think that it is right that even though the number of people in poverty is falling, the gap between the wealthiest and the poorest has not shrunk at all?

Shareholders in China watch share prices on a large screen.

All of the New Global Economies have become wealthier as their economies have grown rapidly. However, the benefits of that economic growth have not been shared equally amongst the people. There have been winners and losers. Poverty still exists and tackling this problem is an important target for all of these countries.

'You grow up in an environment full of **diseases, violence and drugs…** you don't have the right to education, work or leisure, and you are forced to "eat in the hands of the government". You have to accept whatever they give you.'
Padre Jordano, a young woman living in a slum area of Brazil, 2006

Poverty in the New Global Economies

The World Bank defines extreme poverty as having to live on less than $1.00 a day and moderate poverty as living on $2.00 a day. In India it is estimated that about 27% of the population lives below the poverty line. That fell from 51% in 1977 and 36% in 1993, but there is still a long way to go. India has more children suffering from malnutrition than any other country in the world. Brazil is noted as a country that has vast differences between the wealthy and the poor. In 2005, about 30% of the Brazilian population was living below the poverty line. At the same time the richest 10% of Brazilians controlled nearly 45% of the country's wealth.

Tackling poverty in China

In the late 1970s, it was estimated that nearly 65% of China's population lived below the poverty line. As the economic reforms began to have an effect that number began to fall, and by 2004 the number of Chinese people in poverty had fallen to about 10%, but this is still over 130 million people. By contrast, there are about 300,000 households in China that earn over one million dollars per year, and there are 106 billionaires.

Rural and urban

As industries have expanded, people have begun to move from the countryside to the cities in search of a better life. The urban population of India is about 30% and is growing fast. Over the past 20 years, around 200 million people have left the Chinese countryside to head for the cities. Although farming remains a major industry in China, wages are low so many of the young people move to the cities, leaving behind older people. This means that there are not enough people around to do the hard physical work involved in farming.

A farmer with his horse on a field near Novozybkov, Russia. Most of the rural population in the area still live in great poverty.

Workers' rights

One of the main reasons why companies in the developed regions of Europe and North America have opened factories in the New Global Economies is because they can make more money. Wages are lower, there are not as many regulations about how the factory should operate and the workers do not have strong organisations such as trade unions to protect them. This has led to many people questioning whether workers are being exploited.

Protecting workers

Many countries in Europe and North America have laws to protect workers' rights. They make sure that employees are paid a living wage and that safety in their places of work is high enough to protect them from harm. However, in many of the New Global Economies these laws are either very weak or are ignored by many business owners. In both India and China, workers in the Special Economic Zones have to work with less rights than workers in the rest of the country. In Mexico, attempts to create trade unions to protect workers have been blocked, often with the use of violence.

Migrant labourers at work in the Dalian Development Zone, China. These workers have fewer rights than the resident Chinese population.

'When I started with Sony in 1979 there were 25 employees. By 1982 there were 2,000 of us assembling audio and video cassettes. **We wanted a union that was independent** and represented our views, with leaders elected democratically. In April 1994, we had a peaceful demonstration outside the factory to protest. The company brought in fire trucks with water cannons and police with clubs. They beat us badly and there were many injuries.' **Martha Ojeda**, a Mexican trade union activist

> **THOUGHT BOX**
>
> Many people in Europe and North America will not buy goods made in factories that do not treat their workers well. However, that might mean that the workers will lose their jobs. What would you do?

Migrant workers in China

Over the past 20 years, a huge number of Chinese people have left their homes to find work in boom-cities such as Shanghai. These migrant workers do not enjoy the same rights as the natives of Shanghai. They have no rights to an education, pension or welfare and they have to pay a residency permit every year. They are paid very poor wages (about $2.00 a day) and many of them have to live in dormitories with other workers. There is a trade union for Chinese workers. It is called the ACFTU (All-China Federation of Trade Unions). However, this union is part of the ruling Communist Party and cannot act independently.

Safety at work

Safety standards in many factories in the developing world are much lower than in the developed world. In 2002, it was estimated that 140,000 people were killed at work. It is also believed that over 160 million Chinese people work in dangerous conditions.

A worker assembles a Suzuki Maruti car at a factory in the industrial town of Gurgaon, India.

Child labour

For much of the history of the world, children have worked for a living. The rights to an education, to have the opportunity to play or to spend time with their families were denied them. In many of the poorer countries this is still a reality for some children. These countries are attempting to eradicate child labour but widespread poverty means that many families rely on the wages of their children in order to survive. Reducing child labour and poverty go hand in hand.

Child labour in Brazil

In 1992, it was calculated that over 600,000 Brazilian children were working. By 2004, this number had shrunk to just over 200,000. Nearly all of them were either living in shanty towns, called favelas, or were living on the streets. It is illegal for children to work in factories so many children have jobs such as cleaning car windscreens, shining shoes or selling souvenirs to tourists. They also work in the houses of wealthy Brazilians as maids or cleaners.

'I sell craft necklaces to tourists. I got started selling necklaces when I first bought a dozen of them from the people who sell them on…Before selling jewellery, I worked in a fruit market. **Hamilton**, a Brazilian street child who had to work to survive

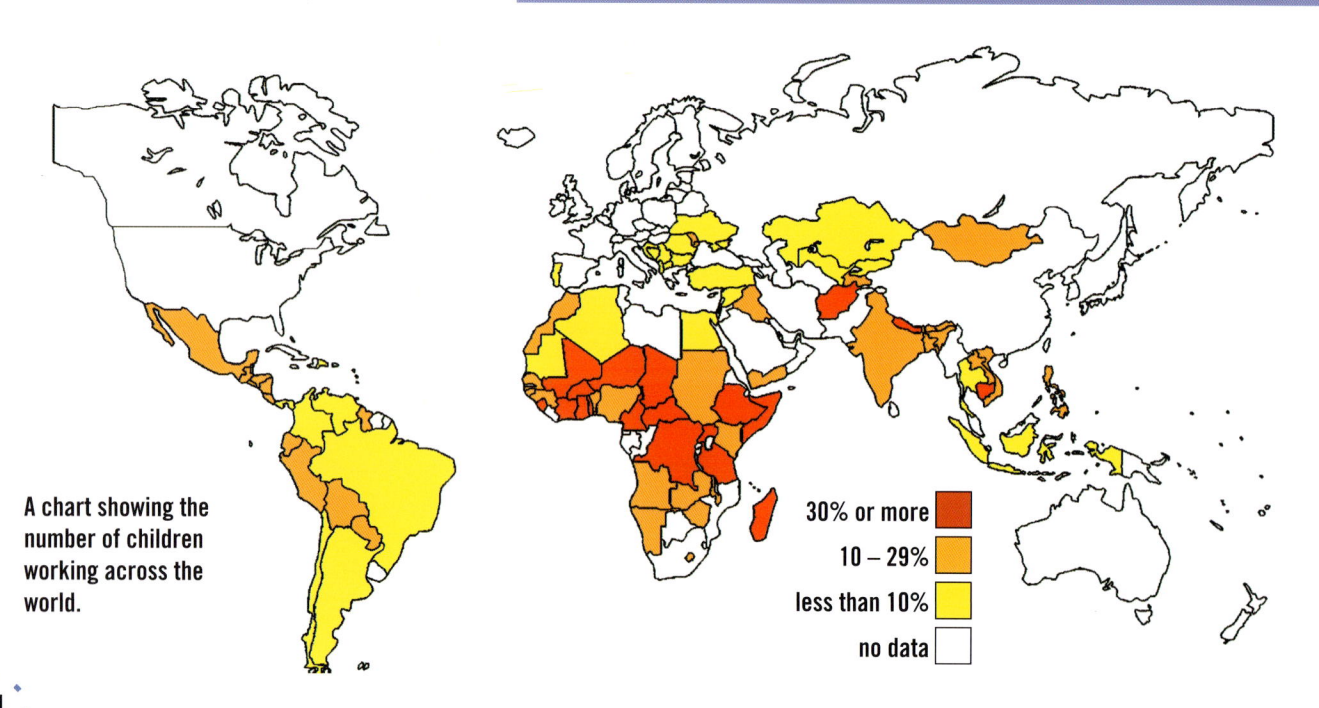

A chart showing the number of children working across the world.

- 30% or more
- 10 – 29%
- less than 10%
- no data

Children work in a stone factory in the village of Visal Pur, India.

Child labour in India

Child labour remains a huge problem in India. There are no reliable figures for the number of children working, but it has been estimated at about 100 million. Children often work for very low wages and in appalling conditions. India also has a problem with child 'bonded labour', a form of modern slavery. This is when poor families are forced through poverty to sell their children to wealthy Indians to work in their homes and businesses.

Child labour in China

China has successfully tackled the issue of child labour. By the end of the 1990s, nearly 99% of all Chinese children were going to school. The fact that poverty in China has been dramatically cut has also meant that child labour is no longer necessary. There are still some small pockets of child labour, particularly among the children of some migrant workers who cannot go to school and so work instead. In rural areas many children work alongside their families on farms.

THOUGHT BOX

Several well-known companies such as Gap and Adidas have sold goods made by child labour in Indian factories, although many of them denied they knew about it. Would you buy something if you knew it was made by a child?

Politics and human rights

Some people feel that it is morally wrong for European and North American companies to do business with countries that are not democracies and that deny their citizens basic human rights. These companies defend their position by saying that, as the new global economies become wealthier, their political systems will open up as well.

A poor man selling newspapers in the city of Delhi, India.

Democracy in the New Global Economies

The governments of Brazil, Mexico and India are democracies. This means that the people vote on a regular basis for the government that they want. In Brazil the president and the parliament are elected and there are four main parties for the people to choose from. India is sometimes called the largest democracy in the world because of the size of the electorate. Mexico also has a democracy but it has been accused of corruption. This is because the same political party was in charge from the 1920s until 1997. However, in each of these countries there have been accusations of human rights abuses. The Mexican police have been accused of using torture and journalists have been killed for criticising the government. The Brazilian police are also suspected of using torture and of killing people that they thought were criminals.

Politics and human rights in China

Although China's economy has gained some freedom over the past few decades, the same cannot be said of China's politics. China is ruled by one party: the Chinese Communist Party. Opposition to this one-party rule is not allowed and freedom of speech in not tolerated. Access to the Internet is restricted and there are many websites that Chinese people are forbidden from viewing. China also executes more people than any other country – about 1,000 people every year.

THOUGHT BOX

The Chinese government argues that the welfare and increased prosperity of all its people is more important than the freedom of individuals. What do you think of this argument?

A Chinese protester holds up tanks during the Tiananmen Square protest, 1989.

The Tiananmen Square protests

In 1989, Communist governments around the world began to lose power. In May 1989 about one million Chinese students and workers occupied Tiananmen Square in Beijing and called for democratic reform. For a whole month it seemed as though the government might give in to their demands. However, on 4 June, the Chinese army was sent in to break up the protest. No one knows how many people were killed – the official figure is 200 but it is thought to be much higher. Many protestors were sent to prison and several others are still missing.

'Past human rights violations like the crackdown on 4 June, 1989, are not erased by the passage of time. Only when **demands for justice** by its own people are addressed can China truly move forward as a responsible member of the international community.'
Sharon Hom, Executive Director of Human Rights in China, 2008

Environmental concerns

Economic growth of a country comes hand in hand with increasing environmental damage. In part this is because the citizens, by becoming wealthier, are buying more cars and products, and using more electricity. In addition, the hunger for raw materials and land for development affects the local environments of the countries as well as the world at large. Huge amounts of damaging greenhouse gases are pumped out of factories to contribute to global warming.

Losing soil

Both India and China are suffering from soil erosion. About 30% of China is desert and rapid industrialisation is causing this area to increase. The expansion of agricultural land to feed the wealthier population and replace land lost to factories, as well as the building of hydroelectric dams has caused the desert to spread. India's forests are also being cut down to make room for farmland and Brazil is clearing its rainforests for agriculture.

Burning Amazonian rainforest in Brazil.

'The world's second-largest **emitter of greenhouse gases** is the People's Republic of China. Yet, China was entirely exempted from the requirements of the Kyoto Protocol. India and Germany are among the top emitters. Yet, India was also exempt from Kyoto.' **US President George W. Bush**, 2006

Creating greenhouse gases

Perhaps the most important environmental problem facing the entire world is climate change, caused by greenhouse gases such as carbon dioxide. The rise in industrialisation and wealth means that the New Global Economies are increasing their greenhouse gas emissions. China produces nearly as much carbon dioxide as the United States and that figure is growing. India is the fourth-largest producer of greenhouse gases in the world. In their defence, these countries claim that they are just trying to achieve the standard of living that Western countries have enjoyed for decades. In addition, if the carbon dioxide emissions are measured per head of population, then the developed Western countries are still the main polluters. An international agreement called the Kyoto Protocol was signed in 1997. It obliged countries around the world to cut their carbon dioxide emissions. Under the protocol, China, India and Brazil did not have to cut their emissions because they were poorer countries.

A new coal-fired power station under construction in China, one of over 500 new coal power plants being built.

THOUGHT BOX

Do you think that China, India and Brazil should be exempt from cutting their greenhouse gases, given the threat to the world created by climate change?

The growth of the city

A crowded commuter train in Mumbai, India.

THOUGHT BOX
Do you think that the governments of the new global economies should try and slow down the growth of their cities until the problems of housing, transport and sewage are sorted out?

As the New Global Economies become wealthier and more industrialised, people have begun to move to find better jobs for themselves and better opportunities for their families. This usually means moving to where these new jobs are and this means the city. For the first time in world history, more people now live in towns and cities than in the countryside.

Moving to the city

In 1990, about 74% of China's population lived in the countryside. Since then that percentage has fallen rapidly as people have moved to the cities. In 2001, it had fallen to 64% and by the end of 2006 the rural population stood at 56%. China is turning into an urban society. In India it is estimated that 30 million people every year are moving from rural to urban areas. The same trend is seen in Brazil and Mexico.

Stresses and strains

Such a rapid movement of people has placed a huge burden on cities. For a city to work properly it needs enough housing, reliable public transport, a good sewage system and enough school places for the children. In all of the New Global Economies, urban growth has been so rapid that it has been almost impossible for cities to provide these essentials. This has led to the growth of shanty towns on the edges of cities, public transport that cannot cope with demand and sewage systems on the point of collapse.

The mega-city

A mega-city is a city with a population of more than 10 million people. In 1950, there were only two cities in the entire world that could be called mega-cities: New York and Tokyo. By 2005, that had grown to 20 cities and the United Nations estimates that this will increase to 22 by 2015. Of those 22 cities, 17 will be in the developing world and 10 will be in the New Global Economies. It will be a challenge for these mega-cities to provide a safe, healthy place to live for millions of urban dwellers.

Migrant workers forced to sleep on the stairs of the metro in Shanghai, China. Around 300 million peasants have moved into China's cities in the last ten years.

'Chongqing is trying to clean up, but this is **a low priority** compared to economic growth. And it is hard to find a place for the ever-expanding waste. We head into the hills to see the biggest of the mega-city's rubbish mega-pits: the Changshengqiao landfill site. It is an awesome sight; a giant reservoir of garbage, more than 30 metres deep and stretching over 350,000 square metres.'
Jonathan Watts writing about China's waste in the *Guardian*, 15 March, 2006

New world powers

As any country becomes more economically powerful it also becomes more important on the world stage. The New Global Economies are beginning to demand more of a say in world affairs. This is particularly true of China, and many people believe that China is becoming a new world superpower.

Zhang Yixhan, China's representative to the UN.

Growing regional powers

Although China and India are becoming more important in world affairs, they are even more powerful in their own regions. For both countries, relations with their close neighbours are of high importance. China has important links with Japan, South Korea and Russia and remains an active supporter of countries such as Myanmar (also called Burma) and North Korea, whose governments are criticised for their bad human rights records. India's main political focus is on its close neighbours, Pakistan, Nepal, China, Bangladesh and Afghanistan.

Demanding a bigger voice

Brazil and Mexico are both beginning to insist that they have a bigger say in what happens in their regions. Both countries are now the most powerful in South and Central America but they are also starting to become bigger players in the whole of America. The United States and Canada have to take more notice of these two countries. Because of its growing economic power and also because it possess nuclear weapons, India is campaigning to have a permanent seat on the United Nations Security Council.

'India is a good example of a powerful country, **the biggest democracy in the world**, that deserves a seat at the top table.'
Gordon Brown, the Prime Minister, supports India's attempts to get a permanent seat on the United Nations Security Council, 2007

> **THOUGHT BOX**
>
> Do you think that we should play less attention to human rights abuses in the New Global Economies if we rely on them economically?

World leaders gather together at the G8 summit in Heiligendamm, Germany, on 7 July, 2007.

Relations with the West

The New Global Economies and the developed world need each other. China and India now provide many of the manufactured goods for the world. Brazil has raw materials, such as iron, that are needed by industry worldwide. The developed world needs to buy these goods and raw materials and the New Global Economies need the developed world to carry on buying them. This means that countries in the developed world are reluctant to criticise the New Global Economies for their actions both at home and around the world.

Looking for resources

To feed their growing industries and to satisfy the demands of their people for a better standard of living, the New Global Economies need natural resources. They need more oil and gas for their cars and power stations, metals like steel for new buildings and copper to make wiring for their growing telecommunications industries. This has led them into competition for natural resources with the countries of the developed world.

A new gas well in Russia operated by the state-owned firm Gazprom.

China's needs

China's rapid industrialisation and the building boom that has gone with it have created a massive demand for various materials around the world. Over 40% of the world's concrete is bought by the Chinese and about 30% of the world's steel is purchased by them as well. The prices of steel, copper and oil have risen sharply as a result of China's demand. And even though China is the fifth-largest producer of oil in the world, it still needs to import about a third of the oil that it uses. To secure future supplies, the Chinese government has set up companies to drill for oil in Venezuela and Sudan.

'China has been courting the governments of these states aggressively, building goodwill by strengthening bilateral trade relations, awarding aid, forgiving national debt, and helping build roads, bridges, stadiums, and harbours. In return, China has **won access to key resources,** from gold in Bolivia and coal in the Philippines to oil in Ecuador and natural gas in Australia.'

David Zweig, Professor of International Politics at Tufts University, 2005

THOUGHT BOX

How do you think the governments of the developed world should react to the demand for natural resources by the New Global Economies?

Indian Prime Minister Manmohan Singh meets Britain's Queen Elizabeth in November 2007.

India's needs

In April 2008, the Indian Prime Minister, Manmohan Singh, attended the first-ever India-Africa Summit. He promised over $500 million in aid to African countries and established new trading agreements between India and African countries. One of the reasons for this summit was India's need for oil. India already gets about 10% of its oil from Nigeria, and this figure is likely to grow. It is estimated that by 2025, India will be the third-largest importer of oil, after the United States and China. In exchange for the oil, India is offering African countries its expertise in information technology and engineering.

Global culture

Many people are now talking about the global economy. This refers to the fact that most economies worldwide used to be separate but are now linked together so that they depend on each other. This certainly describes the relationship between the New Global Economies and the developed economies. Some people are worried that along with the globalisation of economics there will also be a globalisation of culture.

Showing off wealth

As people's earnings rise they inevitably have more money to spend. Many people want others to notice how successful they have become and so they buy expensive, high-quality products. Often the citizens of China, India and Brazil want to copy the lifestyles of people in the United States or Europe. This means that some parts of their traditional culture are being ignored and are in danger of dying out.

McDonald's restaurants have become very popular places to eat in both India and China. There are over 1,000 McDonald's restaurants in China and that figure is growing. They do not serve Chinese food as their menu is the same around the world. Young people in all of the New Global Economies are also turning away from the traditional clothes and music of their parents and grandparents and are wearing Western clothes and listening to Western pop music.

'For families in China, McDonald's is just **part of the world experience,** part of the internet and all the rest of the modern world. It's maybe not for the older generation, but there is a feeling that if their child can eat at McDonald's then he can go out in the world and succeed.'
Professor Noel Watson, Harvard Business School, 2007

> **THOUGHT BOX**
>
> Do you think that it matters if local cultures begin to disappear and everybody starts to wear the same clothes, to listen to the same music and to eat the same food? If you think it does matter, what would you do to preserve these local cultures?

A McDonald's restaurant in the Forum shopping mall in Bangalore, India.

Rising food prices

In India and China, wealthier people are now eating Western-style food. The traditional food of rice is being replaced by wheat-based foods such as bread. This is beginning to have an impact on the price of wheat around the world. Growing demand for wheat-based foods is pushing up the price of wheat worldwide. Chinese officials are concerned that many more Chinese children are eating unhealthy Western foods and the number of children with weight problems and diabetes is increasing.

Beijing youth sport trendy Western hairstyles.

The Spring Festival

In China the Spring Festival is one of the most important events of the year. Chinese people gather together from all over the country to celebrate the start of the Chinese New Year. The Chinese government allows everybody to take a holiday in order to celebrate this festival. However, there are signs that the Spring Festival is changing. The use of fireworks was once common but has been forbidden in many cities. The dumplings and cakes that were eaten as part of the festival have been replaced by bread. Young Chinese people now celebrate the Spring Festival by taking part in a Karaoke evening.

The impact on the developed world

As the economies of the developed world and the New Global Economies are drawn closer together then what happens in India, China, Brazil and Mexico will have more of an impact on the lives of people in Europe and North America. Some of these effects are already being felt by people in the developed world.

Job losses at home

Wages for workers in developing countries are lower than in the developed world, so many Western companies have moved jobs from their own countries to India and China. Out of the top 500 companies in the world, about 400 have set up businesses in China. China builds over 30% of the world's computers, over 60% of microwave ovens and 40% of all televisions. Only a few decades ago many of these products were made closer to home. Meanwhile, call centres in India now handle work that was once based in the UK or other developed countries. Thousands of factories and call centres in the West have cut jobs or closed down completely.

Workers produce Adidas leisure wear at the Shengyuan Clothing Factory in China, which employs 250 workers.

A migrant worker involved in the Olympic Games Village construction site in China.

THOUGHT BOX

How do you think that the rise of the new global economies is benefitting people in the developed world? What are the down sides?

Lower prices

The fact that many manufacturing jobs have moved to India and China has brought one important benefit for consumers in the developed world. As the wages of the workers in the New Global Economies are lower than in the West, the goods that they are making are cheaper in the shops.

Higher prices

However, demand for goods in the New Global Economies is also pushing some prices up. The cost of wheat around the world reached record levels in 2007. Much of this was due to a rising demand from India and China. The costs of raw materials such as concrete, copper and steel are all going up, increasing building costs throughout the world. Demand for oil in the New Global Economies will also drive up the prices of many goods that are bought in the developed world, and the price of petrol and diesel.

'We are seeing a demand curve largely from Asia ... I don't think we have seen this since the 1940s, when there was a global rebuilding effort after World War II.'

Hugh Grant, Chief Executive of Monsanto, talking about the rise in corn and wheat prices, 2008

39

The future

The bank Goldman Sachs has written several reports on the new global economies, particularly the BRIMCs (Brazil, Russia, India, Mexico and China). Their report released in 2005 predicted that by 2050, all five of the BRIMC countries will be in the top seven of the world's largest economies. Only Japan and the United States will also be in this group. What will this mean in the future? What might life be like for people in both the developed world and in the new global economies?

THOUGHT BOX

If you believe that the future belongs to the new global economies, do you think that this is a good or a bad thing for the developed world?

The New Global Economies

At the moment nearly all of what the New Global Economies produce is sold in the developed world. A pair of shoes manufactured in China or India is exported to Europe or North America. However, as people earn more money then it will no longer be necessary to export these products. This will make the New Global Economies much less dependent on the developed world.

Eventually, due to climate change, these countries will probably be obliged to take part in the worldwide effort to reduce their greenhouse gases. They will also become much more important in the international arena. Support for India to become a permanent member of the United Nations Security Council is growing. Several African and Asian countries are pushing for India's membership.

A middle class home in a "condominio", or gated community, in Brazil, built for families worried about the violence in Brazil's capital Sao Paulo.

'China is like a sleeping giant. And when she awakes, she shall astonish the world.' **Napoleon Bonaparte,** the Emperor of France, made this statement in 1803.

Acrobats perform for the Chinese State Circus, 2008.

The developed world

If the countries of the developed world are to meet the challenge of the New Global Economies then some things will probably change in the future. First of all, it is clear that prices for many goods that are cheap at the moment will go up. People in the West will have to pay more for their food, clothing and energy from oil. To protect jobs from moving to China or India, workers in the developed world may have to accept lower wages. Governments will also have to encourage companies to stay by cutting taxes and business regulations. However, companies from the New Global Economies are starting to set up businesses and factories in developed countries and more jobs could be created this way.

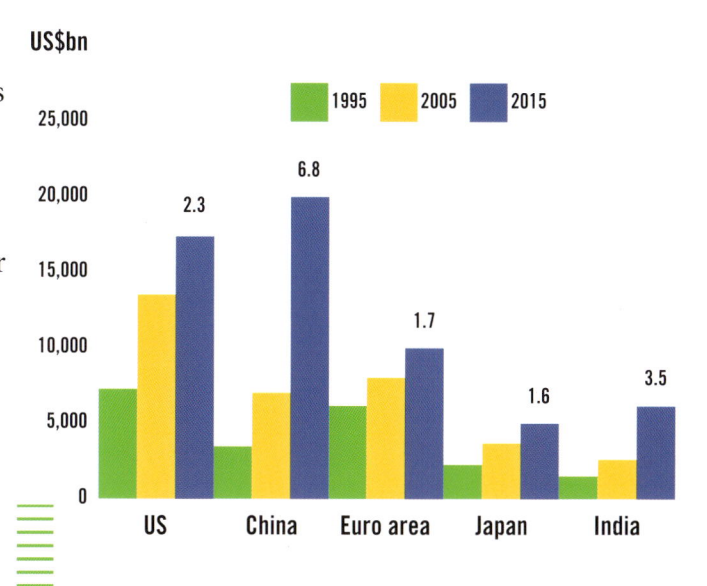

A chart showing the growth of five countries' economies between 1995 and 2005, and the predicted growth by 2015.

Glossary

BRIC The first definition of the main New Global Economies made by the bank Goldman Sachs. It stands for Brazil, Russia, India and China.

BRIMC The most recent definition of the main New Global Economies made by the bank Goldman Sachs. It stands for Brazil, Russia, India, Mexico and China.

Communist A description of the party that currently controls China. It is based on the idea that the economy should be controlled by the state on behalf of the people.

Corruption Dishonest activities.

Consumer Somebody who buys goods with money.

Democracy A system of government in which the adult population of a country are entitled to vote for, and change, the government.

Developed countries Countries that have industrialised and the population have a high standard of living.

Developing countries Countries that are less industrialised and depend more on agriculture. The people of developing countries tend to be poorer than those on developed countries.

Electorate Members of the public with the right to vote.

Free market This is a description of an economy that is free from government regulation and interference. Many of the New Global Economies have only recently become free markets.

Globalisation This word is used to describe the way that the economy of the world is heading. National economies are much more closely tied together through trade, foreign investment and the spread of technology.

Industrialisation This is a process in which the economy of a country moves from being mostly based on agriculture into one which produces goods in factories.

Mega-city A mega-city is a description of a huge city that has more than 10 million inhabitants. By 2015 nearly half of the world's mega-cities will be in the New Global Economies.

Monopoly The exclusive possession or control of something.

New Global Economy The term used in this book to describe those countries with rapid economic and industrial growth. The word 'global' is used because of the impact that they will have on the rest of the world.

Privatisation This is when businesses that were owned by the government are sold to private groups or individuals. Privatisation started in the 1980s in Europe and North America and is still continued in the New Global Economies.

Raw materials These are materials that come from the natural world. This can include metals like steel or copper, wood from trees or oil and gas that is extracted from deep underground.

Urbanisation This is a description of when the population of a country moves from the countryside into cities. Urbanisation and industrialisation are usually linked to each other.

West, the A way of describing countries in Europe and North America or countries that are economically and politically similar to Europe and North America. This can include countries such as Australia and Japan.

Weblinks

https://www.cia.gov/library/publications/the-world-factbook/index.html
The 'World Factbook' is a website maintained by the CIA (Central Intelligence Agency) in the United States. It contains information on every country in the world and includes details of populations, economics and geography. It is useful for finding information on the New Global Economies.

http://news.bbc.co.uk/1/hi/programmes/documentary_archive/4287286.stm
A website linked to series of radio programmes on the BRICs. All of the programmes can be downloaded as MP3 files.

http://www.un.org/esa/desa
This United Nations website has lots of information on world economics in the future.

http://www.worldbank.org
The World Bank website has a lot of information about development around the world. The World Bank provides financial and technological assistance to developing countries.

http://uk.china-embassy.org/eng/cic/t27125.htm
A booklet produced by the Chinese Embassy in the United Kingdom for use in the classroom.

http://en.wikipedia.org/wiki/BRIC
Introduction to the economies of Brazil, Russia, India and China, charting their growing influence on the world.

http://news.bbc.co.uk/1/hi/programmes/documentary-archive/4287124.stm
The BBCs page looking at the changing face of global economic power.

http://www2.goldmansachs.com/ideas/index.html
The bank Goldman Sachs' guide to the BRICS.s

Note to parents and teachers:
Every effort has been made by the Publishers to ensure that these websites are suitable for children, that they are of the highest educational value, and that they contain no inappropriate or offensive material. However, because of the nature of the Internet, it is impossible to guarantee that the contents of these sites will not be altered. We strongly advise that Internet access is supervised by a responsible adult.

Index

Brazil 9, 16, 17, 18, 20-21, 24, 26, 28, 29, 30, 32, 33, 36, 38, 40, 42
BRIC 9, 42
BRIMC 8, 9, 40, 42
Britain see United Kingdom
Bush, George W 29

Canada 8, 32
China 9, 10, 12-13, 15, and throughout
Chongqing 31
cities, growth of 21, 30-31
Cold War 10, 11
Communism 11, 12, 13, 23, 26-27, 42
computers 15, 19, 38
culture 36-37

democracy 26-27, 42
Deng Xiaoping 12, 13

education 18-19, 20, 23, 24, 25
environment 28-29
erosion, soil 28

food 12, 36, 37, 39, 40
France 8, 9, 10, 41

G8 8, 9
gases, greenhouse 28, 29, 40
Germany 8, 9, 29
Goldman Sachs 9, 17, 40, 42

Hong Kong 13

India 9, 10, 14-15, 16, and throughout
industrialisation 28-29, 30, 34, 42
Italy 8, 9

Japan 8, 9, 10, 32, 40, 42
job (losses) 38-39

labour, child 24-25
literacy, levels of 18

Mao Zedong 12
market, free 10-11, 13, 42
materials, raw 28, 33, 34-35, 39, 42
McDonalds 36
mega-cities 31, 42
Mexico 9, 10, 22, 26, 30, 32, 38, 40, 42

oil 34, 35, 39, 41, 42

politics, world 8, 32-33, 40
populations 16-17, 18, 21, 28, 30, 31, 42
  ageing 17
poverty 15, 20-21, 24, 25
privatisation 10, 15, 42
Protocol, Kyoto 29

Rao, Narasimha 15
Regan, Ronald 10
rights, human 26-27, 32, 33

rights', workers 22-23
Russia 8, 9, 11, 16, 32, 40, 42

safety, workplace 22-23
Shanghai 23
Singh, Manmohan 15, 35
South Africa 9
South Korea 9, 32
Soviet Union 11
Summit, India-Africa 35
superpowers 11, 32

technology, information 10, 11, 15, 19, 35
telecommunications 11, 15, 19, 34
Thatcher, Margaret 10
Tiananmen Square 27
towns, shanty 24, 31

unions, trade 22-23
United Nations
  Security Council 32, 40
United Kingdom 8, 9, 10, 13, 14, 18, 38
United States 8, 9, 10, 11, 18, 29, 32, 35, 36, 40
universities 18, 19
urbanisation 21, 30-31, 42

wages 21, 22-23, 24, 25, 38, 39, 41
warming, global 28
workers, migrant 22, 23, 25
workforce 13, 16-17, 19
World War II 11, 39

Zones, Special
  Economic 13, 15, 22, 23

44